Tig Chinese Horoscope 2024

By
IChingHun FengShuisu

Copyright © 2024 By IChingHun FengShuisu
All rights reserved

Table of Contents

Introduce 5

Year of the TIGER (Earth) | (1938) & (1998) 8

    Overview 8

    Career and Business 10

    Financial 11

    Family 12

    Love 13

    Health 14

Year of the TIGER (Golden) | (1950) & (2010) 15

    Overview 15

    Career and Business 17

    Financial 18

    Family 19

    Love 19

    Health 20

Year of the TIGER (Water) | (1962) 22

    Overview 22

    Career and Business 23

    Financial 24

    Family 25

    Love 26

    Health 27

Year of the TIGER (Wood) | (1974) 28

    Overview 28

    Career and Business 30

    Financial 32

    Family 33

Love..34

Health..35

Year of the TIGER (Fire) | (1986)..36

Overview...36

Career and Business..38

Financial...39

Family...40

Love...41

Health...41

Chinese Astrology Horoscope for Each Month............................42

Month 12 in the Rabbit Year (6 Jan 24 - 3 Feb 24)...............42

Month 1 in the Dragon Year (4 Feb 24 - 5 Mar 24).............45

Month 2 in the Dragon Year (6 Mar 24 - 5 Apr 24).............47

Month 3 in the Dragon Year (6 Apr 24 - 5 May 24).............47

Month 4 in the Dragon Year (6 May 24 - 5 Jun 24).............49

Month 5 in the Dragon Year (6 Jun 24 - 6 Jul 24)...............51

Month 6 in the Dragon Year (7 Jul 24 - 7 Aug 24)...............53

Month 7 in the Dragon Year (8 Aug 24 - 7 Sep 24).............56

Month 8 in the Dragon Year (8 Sep 24 - 7 Oct 24).............58

Month 9 in the Dragon Year (8 Oct 24 - 6 Nov 24).............61

Month 10 in the Dragon Year (7 Nov 24 - 6 Dec 24)..........63

Month 11 in the Dragon Year (7 Dec 24 - 5 Jan 24)...........66

Amulet for The Year of the TIGER..69

4

Introduce

The character of people born in the year of the TIGER

You are a brave, fearless, competitive individual who is willing to go through both your brains and the force. Because you are optimistic, a leader, and intelligent, people are drawn to you. Tigers are generous, but if they are bullied, they will become scolded and violent. In terms of work and finances, the tiger was born to be the lord of the jungle, with its kingdom deep within, so you don't like being a subordinate, money isn't a big deal, and prestige is more important, even if it's difficult to achieve. You will not submit to someone you do not respect. If you work and your boss does not respect you, you will resign and look for another job immediately.

You are not a greedy person who enjoys collecting money and living a comfortable life in which happiness is always available. There is no need to work hard and then spend money on happiness to compensate later. You're always generous to your friends, but if someone doesn't talk to your ears, you'll lose them. You're also ready to smoke out of your ears if a long-term partner knows you're easily irritated and recover quickly. Your new friends, on the other hand, will be taken aback. Nothing at all. You take love seriously. Love someone who truly loves you, but quickly grows bored and enters love textbooks, and when you break up, you can find someone new very quickly.

Strength:
Others admire you for your willingness to assist others.

Weaknesses:
You are as impatient as a tiger and refuse to listen to anyone who encourages you to hurt yourself.

Love:
The majority of Tigers are very people who enjoy allowing others to love themselves. People born in this year are often very selective and do not have a particular love for anyone.

They sometimes choose too many things until they have nothing left. However, with charming words, some easily fall in love with the Tiger. If you think you're going to deceive, you'll have to plan carefully because people born this year are very smart. Because you're constantly meeting new people, it's easy to fall in love with people from all over.

Suitable Career:
Planting trees, landscaping, making wooden furniture, trading wood, selling flowers, and stationery, selling books, publishing, printing houses, selling paper, novelists, teachers, opening a pharmacy, selling tea leaves, or occupations related to herbs such as selling cosmetics with herbs as an ingredient, making spas, selling fabrics, plastics, or equipment related to worshiping gods or telecom And businesses involving import-export, dealing with foreigners, and so on are all appropriate for those born in the year of the Tiger.

Year of the TIGER (Earth) | (1938) & (1998)

"The TIGER in the stall" is a person born in the year of the TIGER at the age of 86 years (1938) and 26 years (1998)

Overview

There are no challenges for senior fortune tellers around this age in the broader picture of commerce, trade, and money. This year, the most essential thing to remember is to take care of your own health. Because these are the days of relaxing and caring for one's own health. Because you have a high risk of developing problems. As a result, you should choose to consume clean and sanitary food, have an annual health check, and consult a doctor right away if you notice any strange symptoms. If you have the time, find a way to produce merit, create merit, pray consistently, and pay honor to the Buddha. It will assist you in feeling cheerful, serene, and letting go. Then, at the end of life, you will only discover bliss.

For young individuals around the age of 26, the Year of the Tiger is considered a fortunate year in which money, prosperity, and support will come to assist you. There are also favorable moments for those of you who have a companion. It is a good time to propose love, get engaged, marry, start a family, and it is also a good time to expand work, grow business or establish a store, start your own business, build up, and settle down. This is due to the lucky star "Leng Tek" circling and shining brilliantly in your destiny house this year. This is the year to move on with any project or invest in numerous enterprises. You will see growth and economic expansion since it has the auspicious power to assist and promote effort. However, you must be cautious of the impacts of the evil star that will torment you, notably the "Huang Puai Star," which will extend its influence and damage you in matters of treachery. A conflict or a disagreement occurs. As a result, you should be careless in order to avoid barriers and issues that may arise over the year.

Career and Business

This year's work and business strategy gives you the opportunity to demonstrate your abilities. Diligence and determination will help you acquire the trust of your elders. Have faith in the next great thing. The months for starting a new job, entering stocks, and making various investments this year include the 2nd Chinese month (5 Mar. - 3 Apr.), the 6th Chinese month (6 Jul. - 6 Aug.), the 7th Chinese month (7 Aug. - 6 Sep.), and the 10th Chinese month (7 Nov. - 5 Dec.). If you wish to accomplish it, you should seek counsel. Consult a qualified guru or an adult with prior expertise. Because proper counsel will help your investments avoid losses. However, you should exercise caution during the months when work and trade will present obstacles and problems that you must overcome, such as the 1st Chinese month (4 Feb. - 4 Mar.), the third Chinese month (4 April - 4 May), the fifth Chinese month (5 June - 5 July), and the eighth Chinese month (7 September - 7 October). You should avoid investing during this time period. Because there is a danger of getting duped. Insiders or partners may also be corrupt. Furthermore, before entering into a contract to obtain a scholarship or take a job, you should carefully review the contract's terms. There may be certain things that may bring you harm and issues in the future. There may be certain things that will injure you and give you troubles in the future.

Financial

This year's financial situation is rich ground. As a result, it is an excellent moment to work hard, put money in your pocket, and learn how to collect savings as capital in order to advance towards a bright future. It is also a source of funds for investment in order to increase profitability. Especially during the months when your funds will flow freely, such as the 2nd Chinese month (5 Mar. - 3 Apr.), the 6th Chinese month (6 Jul. - 6 Aug.), the 7th Chinese month (7 Aug. - 6 Sep.), and the 10th Chinese month (7 Nov. - 5 Dec.), gambling will not bring in much money. Some are arriving at specific times. However, you should not wager much because it will not be worthwhile. Take cautious not to be overly greedy. Your riches will usually vanish. These are the months when your money may be challenging and you should be cautious about investing: The 1st Chinese month (4 Feb. - 4 Mar.) The 3rd Chinese month (4 Apr - 4 May) 5th Chinese month (5 Jun. - 5 Jul.) and 8th Chinese month (7 Sep. - 7 Oct). Never lend money to others or make financial pledges to assist others. You should avoid engaging in commercial endeavors that are likely to violate the law or copyrights since you may be charged with a crime.

Family

This year will provide you auspicious energy inside your household. There are conditions in the house for conducting auspicious occasions. Both will welcome more new members. But be wary of the evil star that takes over the family base and causes internal strife. There will almost always be disagreements and conflicts. As a result, you must avoid turning little issues into major ones. Especially during the 1st Chinese month (4 Feb. - 4 Mar.), the 3rd Chinese month (4 Apr. - 4 May), the 5th Chinese month (5 Jun. - 5 Jul.), and the 8th Chinese month (7 Sep. - 7 Oct.). Be wary of subordinates who cause problems during this time. You should also be wary about valuables being destroyed, lost, or stolen.

Love

Overall, the love horoscope for this year appears to be very smooth. Those who are destined to be single this year have a good chance of finding love. The opposite sex will be particularly curious and eager to meet new people. Because you will be gorgeous and fascinating. Let's study together gradually, those of you who are studying with each other. However, if you are certain, you can apply to become your life partner. However, you should use caution during the months when difficulties are likely to arise: The 1st Chinese month (4 Feb. - 4 Mar.), the 3rd Chinese month (4 Apr. - 4 May), the 5th Chinese month (5 Jun. - 5 Jul.), and the 8th Chinese month (7 Sep. - 7 Oct.) Be cautious and check with your emotions to determine whether it is serious or simply flirting for fun. It is improper to deceive the other party if there is a lack of sincerity. As a result, rather than having the other person fall in love and then be disappointed, you should communicate yourself plainly. However, if you are serious, you must act quickly. Because there were others waiting for the right opportunity to act.

Health

This year's health issues are modest. There may be a few mild ailments. If you desire a robust physique, you should exercise more than four times a week for 20 minutes each time. This will be sufficient to assist boost your body's resilience against sickness. But what I'm concerned about this year is showing off or showing off. Be cautious not to make people envious and allow them to mistreat you. This year, you are quite likely to get harmed in a car accident. As a result, you must be extra cautious in everything you do. The months that you should be especially careful include the 1st Chinese month (4 Feb. - 4 Mar.), the 3rd Chinese month (4 Apr. - 4 May), the 5th Chinese month (5 Jun. - 5 Jul.) and the 8th month of

China (7 Sep. - 7 Oct.). If you drink alcohol, you should definitely not drive a vehicle.

Year of the TIGER (Golden) | (1950) & (2010)

" The TIGER journey" is a person born in the year of the TIGER at the age of 74 years (1950) and 14 years (2010)

Overview

Because the planets rotating into his destiny house this year are "Dao Leng Tek," the senior destiny lord is about 74 years old. This year is the year you will get favorable energy to boost your profession and wealth. Throughout the year, you will have the chance to travel both nationally and overseas, as well as participate in merit-making and charitable events. However, elders must continue to be cautious and sensitive to their own health. Always keep your doctor's visits and take your medications as directed. You should also know how to let go. Don't overthink or worry yourself to the point of becoming bedridden.

Even for the kids of this age range, this is an excellent year for academic advancement. However, you must pull your heart to be persistent and resolute in your studies. Don't get disheartened by the stimulation and temptations of technology. This is due to the appearance of the wicked stars Huang Pui and Lok Heung in the house of fate, which orbited to disturb and disturb. This will extend its impact, resulting in the fate owner being easily distracted and lacking attention, and so easily led astray. This year, the mind is like a monkey, like a horse, flying and inquisitive. The terrifying thing is being lured into vice or down an awful road by terrible people. However, it is considered lucky that the auspicious constellations "Leng Tek," "Hok Chae," and "Sam Tai" emerged throughout the year, all circling to provide favorable energy to aid. Enough to assist bring the mind back from being diverted to some amount or thinking that has veered off course, it will do so swiftly. To suppress incorrect ideas, the remainder must utilize conscience and accuracy. However, you must be cautious this year to avoid being caught in the crossfire and being duped into being a tool for criminals to convince you to do something bad.

.

Career and Business

This year, the chosen person's work and education will have auspicious power assisting them to achieve easy advancement in both life cycles. This is because the work foundation has fortunate constellations spinning around it to support and encourage it. As a result of having competent staff to support you in your task, your work and business will thrive. Youth will discover that by studying, they will gain comprehension and be able to score high. But don't be casual about the terrible constellations that will bother you and drive you to become fascinated with a certain issue to the point of losing concentration. The intellect is dispersed and inquisitive. Some stories are also worth examining. However, in many circumstances, it is safer not to attempt. The 1st Chinese month (4 Feb. - 4 Mar), the 3rd Chinese month (4 Apr. - 4 May), the 5th Chinese month (5 Jun. - 5 Jul) and the 8th Chinese month (7 Sep - 7 Oct.) are not supportive and your destiny must be more cautious. Be cautious when organizing a group to go out. You may argue and get caught in the crossfire, or you may incur misfortune as a result of your involvement in an unlawful situation. This will land you and your family in hot water.

Financial

This year's financial fortune is built on earning little and paying a lot. However, learning how to save and save is training to become used to saving money. So utilize less than you take in. Spending extravagantly until you are in the red will cause you to lose sight of your future. Particularly during the months when finances are at risk of becoming stuck and lacking liquidity, namely month 1st Chinese month (4 Feb. - 4 Mar.), 3rd Chinese month (4 Apr. - 4 May), 5th Chinese month (5 Jun. - 5 Jul.), and 8th Chinese month (7 Sep. - 7 Oct.), others are prohibited from lending money or signing financial guarantees.

Family

This year's family will go through both happy and difficult times. Because an evil star has emerged in this base's orbit. You should consequently use caution when it comes to home security. There will be family feuds that will disrupt the tranquility. The 1st Chinese month (4 February - 4 March), the 3rd Chinese month (4 Apr.- 4 May), the 5th Chinese month (5 Jun. - 5 Jul.), and the 8th Chinese month (7 Sep. - 7 Oct.) are the months when troubles and confusion will arise inside the family. Pay special attention to the health of the people in the family at this time. Keep an eye out for persons in the house who are having problems or arguments with those around. Be wary of youngsters or subordinates who cause mischief or cause damage or loss of goods.

Love

In this year's life cycle, the love bond between the two destinies is mild. Seniors will also receive affection and attention from their partners and children. You might be able to participate in activities honoring the Buddha.

Make merit, generate merit, or join forces on a journey.

For teens, heterosexual love is still ambiguous at this time. Making friends initially is not a terrible idea. Please don't think too hastily, like a horse who has wandered off its course, for the day is yet young. Be wary of losing your education and future too soon. During the months of the 1st Chinese month (4 Feb. - 4 Mar.) and the 3rd Chinese month (4 Apr. - 4 May), the 5th Chinese month (5 Jun - 5 Jul) and the 8th Chinese month (7 Sep - 7 Oct), you must be alert and know how to demonstrate a lot of self-preservation. You should avoid being duped by the other side. You may also be duped into loving and then abandoning someone.

Health

This year's destined person's health is poor in both life cycles. Seniors, beware of sleeplessness brought on by stress or other factors. Maintain boundaries when it comes to drinking, eating, and smoking habits. Beware of sicknesses that may occur as a result of giving in to your wishes. Be aware of quiet disorders that appear to interfere and create sickness. You should constantly be aware of any changes in your body and visit your doctor on a yearly basis. When it comes to the health of this year's youngsters, don't ignore safety. Whether it's arranging extracurricular activities or participating in sports outside of the classroom. Including being recruited to join an outside gang and maybe clashing with other organizations. Because stray rounds might cause harm and blood loss. During the months of the 1st Chinese month (4 Feb. - 4 Mar.), the 3rd Chinese month (4 Apr. - 4 May.), the 5th Chinese month (5 Jun. - 5 Jul.), and the 8th Chinese month (7 Sep. - 7 Oct.), individuals in both age cycles should pay extra attention to their health and safety.

Year of the TIGER (Water) | (1962)

" The TIGER is still standing" is a person born in the year of the TIGER at the age of 62 years (1962)

Overview

Around the age of 62, your senior's horoscope will be "Lok Heung Star," which will assist encourage management in the proper way. It aids in the resolution of disagreements in the management line. Work will be completed, and company will flourish. Sales will grow, but they will not stop. You will receive what is said. However, you must act. Increase your effort and diligence to obtain these items. Smoothness is simply promoted by auspicious stars. In terms of finances, you must rely on yourself.

This year, the big picture is looking up, but you'll need to lobby hard, or find a successor or helper to help you progressively spread the job. Throughout the year, there will be possibilities for new investments with excellent returns. However, you cannot be careless about the terrible stars "dangerous planets" that arise during the year, which will result in meeting individuals who want to gain from you, whether it is investing or misleading you into other things. make you lose money Be cautious of health issues. Unexpected incidents might cause you to be hurt for a variety of reasons. This year, you should be cautious and as safe as possible.

Career and Business

In terms of the direction of your job and business, this year is a good time to identify an heir to intern to take over the task or possibly teach him experience in investment management. Even though you are a new generation, you feel that if you join forces with individuals who have expertise, your job or investment will be a spectacular success. Furthermore, the 2nd Chinese month (5 Mar. - 3 Apr.) and the 6th Chinese month (6 Jul. - 6 Aug.) are the months that support and encourage commerce and company success. 7th Chinese month (7 Aug. - 6 Sep.) and 10th Chinese month (7 Nov. - 5 Dec). However, there are some months of the year when work may be difficult, and you should use caution. Investment subjects include the 1st Chinese month (4 February - 4 March), the 3rd Chinese month (4 April - 4 May), the 5th Chinese month (5 Jun. - 5 Jul.), and the 8th Chinese month (7 Sep. - 7 Oct.). Keep an eye out for insiders or partners that conduct fraud or manipulate accounting statistics. You should also use caution in your interactions with clients, business partners, and people you must always contact. Misunderstandings or unhappiness may arise, resulting in confrontation and an inability to look at each other. You should be wary of getting duped out of money during this period.

Financial

Financially, the first half of this year has been promising. After the middle of the year, one must be wary of unexpected intrusion. It will suck money into the system until it becomes stalled and lacks liquidity. Especially in the months when the financial stars are falling. Finances are likely to falter and produce issues during the 1st Chinese month (4 Feb. - 4 Mar.), the 3rd Chinese month (4 Apr. - 4 May), the 5th Chinese month (5 Jun. - 5 Jul.), and the 8th Chinese month (7 Sep. - 7 Oct.). As a result, you should not lend money to anyone or make promises to anybody. Do not be greedy or covet what does not belong to you. Make sure you really want him. Instead, it is possible that we will lose our fortune. You should also avoid participating in or investing in illicit companies. Don't take excellent and quick results for granted. Because you may not be able to avoid both litigation and fines for infringing on the rights of others. The months in which funds have recovered and flowed easily are the 2nd Chinese month (5 Mar. - 3 Apr.), the 6th Chinese month (6 Jul. - 6 Aug.), the 7th Chinese month (7 Aug. - 6 Sep.), and the 10th Chinese month (7 Nov. - 5 Dec.).

Family

This year will be a roller coaster ride for your family's fortunes, but you'll get through it. Be cautious; there might be misunderstandings among the residents or anything wrong with not looking at each other. This year is favorable for relocating to a new home or apartment. There will be a chance to greet new house members. If the house can manage more auspicious happenings this year. It will aid in dispelling the force of misfortune and reducing the misfortune of losing things. However, you should exercise caution during the months when family issues and unrest are likely, such as the first Chinese month (4 February - 4 March), the third Chinese month (4 April - 4 May), the fifth Chinese month (June 5 - July 5) and the eighth Chinese month (7 September - 7 October). You should be cautious against having your things damaged, lost, or stolen. You should strengthen your security measures. Make your house safe and secure, including protecting it from cybercriminals.

Love

This year's love story is on the mild side. Your relationship with each other is still going strong. When you are stuck and experiencing difficulties, you will receive support and assistance from your loved ones. Both have the option of going on sightseeing tours or attending merit-making events together. However, there are some seasons of the year when love is vulnerable, and elders should be cautious of falling victim to the enticements of transient love outside the family, such as the 1st Chinese month (4 Feb. - 4 Mar.), the 3rd Chinese month (4 Apr. – 4 May), 5th Chinese month (5 Jun. – 5 Jul.) and 8th Chinese month (7 Sep. – 7 Oct.). You must be forceful and in command. Your personal actions, don't be unfaithful until you're unable to retreat since it will bring family strife. Avoid going to evening entertainment establishments as well.

Health
This year's physical health is not excellent. It is quite simple to develop health issues. Reduce your intake of too hot and too cold components in particular. That is, it should not be too heavy on one side and should avoid all sorts of hot food, whether salty, sweet, spicy, or highly rich in fat. Because there will be stomach, intestinal, liver, and heart issues this year. If you have time during the year, you should see a doctor for a health checkup. You will be able to behave

properly and take medication as directed by your doctor. minimize the amount of medicine you buy for yourself in order to assist minimize the number of diseases that may arise. The 1st Chinese month (4 Feb. - 4 Mar.), the 3rd Chinese month (4 Apr. - 4 May), the 5th Chinese month (5 Jun. - 5 Jul.), and the 8th Chinese month (7 Sep. - 7 Oct.) are all times to be extra cautious and keep an eye out for any abnormalities in the body, such as repeated pain at any point. If you see regular bleeding or a lump, you should contact a doctor right once for a diagnosis and treatment. Don't leave it for too long or it will be tough to treat.

Year of the TIGER (Wood) | (1974)
" The TIGER in the Mountain" is a person born in the year of the TIGER at the age of 50 years (1974)

Overview
This age cycle is for the Year of the Tiger horoscope since the planet that circles into your horoscope this year is Leng Tek. This year

is thus another good year in which you will receive prosperity, prestige, rank, and renown all at the same time. We only ask that you be determined, determined, and diligent in developing yourself to stay up with the trends. Dare to go out and seize what awaits you. Everything said above will work in your favor. This is because your destiny house has experienced several lucky constellations in your life cycle this year. Dao Leng Tek, Dao Sam Tai, and Dao Hok Chae all promote all job or company operations to go well. Just think about it, and the task will be nearly finished. The problem is in your heart, and the stars are aligned in your favor. You will also receive assistance from your sponsors. However, in this year's house of fate, a collection of evil stars appears to be orbiting together to focus on the influence, including the stars Xiao Ae, Huang Pui, and Kiab Sua. This will cause challenges in staff management, resulting in pandemonium. People in the organization have disagreements, and subordinates are frequently rebellious and seldom execute directions, resulting in blunders in corporate operations and commercial harm. It also appears that certain employees are surreptitiously impeding the sawing of chair legs. You will also encounter corruption and abuse of your own interests. You must be cautious with your words and stance this year. Especially in terms of interpersonal skills. Take cautious not to insult others without realizing it. Others will be irritated and disliked as a result. Be wary of jealous persons who intend to betray you and cause difficulties in your job with working people. As a result, every employment activity you undertake should be evaluated in terms of your own talents. Don't breathe through someone else's nose. Some things may not go as planned. If you must wait, wait till the proper time arrives to exact your wrath to the best of your ability.

Career and Business

Even though three auspicious constellations are orbiting to promote your career and business this year, you cannot underestimate the impact of the evil stars that are involved in your fate because in good or prosperous times, you can't go all the way, you have to watch out for everything. The most essential issue to focus on this year is people management because if you ignore both the boss level and the subordinate level, you may experience problems that hinder your job from progressing, such as clients migrating to buy products or utilize services elsewhere. As a result, when solving difficulties, you must use caution. During the months when work will have a lot of problems and personal obstacles, they include the 1st Chinese month (4 Feb. - 4 Mar.), the 3rd Chinese month (4 Apr. - 4 May), the 5th Chinese month (5 Jun - 5 Jul) and the 8th Chinese month (7 Sep. - 7 Oct.). As for the months in which work and business have improved, they are the 2nd Chinese month (5 Mar. – 3 Apr.), 6th Chinese month (6 Jul. – 6 Aug.), 7th Chinese month (7 Aug. – 6 Sep.), and 10th Chinese month (7 Nov. – 5 Dec.) However, investing in stocks, including diverse assets, is a good way to start a new employment. This year has not been kind to me. Because there is a possibility of being duped into losing money, as well as corruption and embezzlement of insiders.

Financial

This year's finances are generally solid and passable, but be wary of leaks and asset losses. As a result, if your destiny requires further investments in numerous areas, you must exercise caution. You may have an unforeseen incident that causes your finances to falter, or some bad debts may develop, or the debtor may experience a difficulty of not being able to pay on time, or you may be impacted by criminals' trickery, generating business troubles. Especially during the months when finances will face difficulties and a lack of liquidity, such as the 1st Chinese month (4 Feb. - 4 Mar.), the 3rd Chinese month (4 Apr. - 4 May), the 5th Chinese month (5 Jun. - 5 Jul.), and the 8th Chinese month (7 Sep. - 7 Oct.), where the lord of destiny must exercise caution in investing. Don't be a snob. Beware of financial corruption by subordinates or subordinates. Be wary of persons who try to con you into investing in unsafe or unlawful ventures. Also, don't lend money to others or sign financial commitments. As for the months where finances are flowing smoothly, they are the 2nd Chinese month (5 Mar. - 3 Apr.), the 6th Chinese month (6 Jul. - 6 Aug.), the 7th Chinese month (7 Aug. – 6 Sept.) and the 10th Chinese month (7 Nov. – 5 Dec.)

Family

Even if fortunate influences are faced, the family's horoscope will experience both good and negative occurrences. However, he acquired bad power delivered from the evil constellation to destroy him. This frequently has an impact on home safety and health issues. Especially during the months when your house will be in a state of upheaval, such as the 1st Chinese month (4 Feb. - 4 Mar.), the 3rd Chinese month (4 Apr. - 4 May), and the 5th Chinese month (5 Jun. - 5 Jul.) and the 8th Chinese month (7 Sep. - 7 Oct.) give special attention to family members' health and safety. This includes being cautious of valuables being destroyed or lost. But there is also good fortune amid adversity. This year will bring you numerous fortunate events, such as an excellent time to move into a new home or business. The house may get new members.

There may also be favorable occurrences taking place in the residence.

.

Love

This year's love is not as easy as you had hoped. It is due to the encounter of two terrible stars, the Huang Pui star and the Xiao Ae star, both of which circle into the love base. This will cause you to be annoyed on a frequent basis. As a result, the relationship is close. But it appears to be far away. It's like meeting two distinct persons. Both have the capacity to easily produce disputes and confrontations with each other, ranging from little to major issues. Especially during this month, when love is most frail. You must be cautious of disputes that may easily lead you to be at odds with each other, such as the 1st Chinese month (4 Feb. - 4 Mar.), the 3rd Chinese month (4 Apr. - 4 May), the 5th Chinese month (5 Jun. - 5 Jul.), and the 8th Chinese month (7 Sep. - 7 Oct.). Avoid visiting evening entertainment places. Because it will be the catalyst for love, sickness will follow.

Health

Regarding the chosen person's physical health, despite confronting both Dao Xiao Ae and Kiab Sua who stretched their influence to target this base. This causes health and safety issues for you and your family. However, there is a way to mitigate the affliction by having the person of fate pay obeisance to the Buddha, make merit, produce merit, and amass good acts. It will aid in the dispelling of negative energy by stimulating the fortunate energy of Hok Chae and Leng Tek. It will assist in reducing the problem from heavy to light. However, you should be cautious during the following months, when you should pay special attention to your health: the 1st Chinese month (4 Feb. - 4 Mar.), the 3rd Chinese month (4 Apr. - 4 May), the 5th Chinese month (5 Jun. - 5 Jul.), and the 8th Chinese month (7 Sep. - 7 Oct.). You must be cautious of the risks associated with driving a car on the road. Traveling and operating various vehicles must be done with caution.

Year of the TIGER (Fire) | (1986)
" The TIGER in the Forest" is a person born in the year of the TIGER at the age of 38 years (1986)

Overview
For the Year of the Tiger, the planet that circles into your destiny home is "Lok Heung Star" when backed by fortunate energy. This year is thus another excellent year for gaining fortune and reputation, even if work may provide some challenges. However, there are certain portions that are not harmed. It is claimed that the investment is not squandered. Even if certain components were losing money, your attentiveness resulted in a net profit. Your work has been accepted. Many more individuals will trust you and bring employment to you in the future. You will satisfy the criterion if you are dedicated and determined in your aims and do not give up or become disheartened by hurdles that arise. The more work you do, the more money you'll

make. Please examine the opportunities and proper timing that come your way this year. You must also have the bravery to invest in a previously predicted business in order for things to go as planned. It is about growing and raising one's standing to a higher degree. However, even if there are favorable stars and auspicious dates to support it. But, before you decide to invest, don't forget to assess your own readiness in terms of funds, expertise, and staff. Manpower, in particular, is critical at this time. If you don't have the arms and legs to complete a large business or project on your own, it will most likely fail. As a result, the Lord of Fate must hire a trustworthy aide. It is qualified for the job and possesses transferable abilities. When you have finished all of these tasks, you will be on your way to future success. However, several malevolent constellations arose during the year, annoying and impeding efforts. Your interpersonal skills are something you should be aware of and mindful of this year. If there is a lack of correction and improvement, or if sloppy language is used. That is, making more enemies who have the right to be harassed, hampered, or even held accountable, and who will be a barrier to professional development.

Career and Business

Overall, the destined person's career and business are heading in the right route this year. There is a way forward. If you have endurance, dedication, diligence, diligence, and progress gathering, your progress will become tangible and your business will expand. There are two things you should be mindful of: your posture and your speech. As a result, if you want to have numerous triumphs, you must work together to transform to something better. Especially during the months when there will be many hurdles and troubles at work, such as the first Chinese month (4 Feb. - 4 Mar.), the 3rd Chinese month (4 Apr. - 4 May), the 5th Chinese month (5 Jun. - 5 Jul.), and the 8th Chinese month (7 Sep. - 7 Oct.). The fortune teller should use better etiquette and words. Humility is required while communicating with others. Elders will be nice and encouraging. If you meet the requirements to sign any contract paperwork, During this time, one must be diligent in the details. Because there is a set of requirements for being duped into being at a disadvantage.

The months in which the destined person's profession and business are exceptional and progressing are the 2nd Chinese month (5 Mar. - 3 Apr.) and the 6th Chinese month (6 Jul. - 6 Aug.), 7th Chinese months (7 Aug. - 6 Sep.) and 10th Chinese months (7 November - 5 December).

Financial

Overall, the financial horoscope for this year is favorable. Regular revenue from selling items or services, as well as extra money from extra employment and windfalls, will all contribute to cash inflows. But don't be rash. In order to make more money, you must properly handle your finances. The financial luckiest months are the 2nd Chinese month (5 Mar. - 3 Apr.), the 6th Chinese month (6 Jul. - 6 Aug.), the 7th Chinese month (7 Aug. - 6 Sep.), and the 10th Chinese month (7 Nov. - 5 Dec.). There should be a plan in place to assist the aspect of joining stocks and investing. Don't rush to invest based on the market. Because they arrive and depart swiftly. However, if yours is one step slower, you will suffer a loss. Financial troubles will occur during the 1st Chinese month (4 Feb. - 4 Mar.), the 3rd Chinese month (4 Apr. - 4 May), the 5th Chinese month (5 Jun. - 5 Jul.), and the 8th Chinese month (7 Sep.- 7 Oct.). Investing must be done with extreme caution. Furthermore, close relatives should not be permitted to borrow money or sign financial assurances.

Family

Overall, the situation is calm. If your residence has the ability to host auspicious events this year, patronage will come your way. It will help alleviate some of the calamity. However, if there is no auspicious occasion, the malevolent stars that are focused on it will strike. What you should be cautious of are aging health issues in the house and the safety of family members. Especially during the 1st Chinese month (4 Feb. - 4 Mar.), the 3rd Chinese month (4 Apr. - 4

May), the 5th Chinese month (5 Jun. - 5 Jul.), and the 8th Chinese month (7 Sep. - 7 Oct.). Be wary about valuables being destroyed, lost, or stolen. You should be careful of domestic disputes. Because harmony in the home brings wealth and good fortune to everyone.

.

Love

Don't be a fool and go out of your way to become infatuated with fleeting love to the point of causing issues for your family. You must be more cautious in the next months: The first Chinese month (4 February - 4 March), the third Chinese month (4 April - 4 May), the fifth Chinese month (5 June - 5 July), and the eighth Chinese month (7 September - 7 October) should be cautious of quarrels and confrontations that grow into a major issue. Also, do not intervene or act as a third party in the relationships of other couples.

Health

This year, despite the presence of malignant stars in this base, general physical condition is poor. As a result, you cannot afford to be cavalier with the possibility of harm and bloodshed. You should pay great care to your health in the next months, especially: 1st Chinese month (4 Feb. - 4 Mar.), 3rd Chinese month (4 Apr. - 4 May.), and 5th Chinese month (5 Jun. - 5 Jul) and the 8th Chinese month (7 Sep - 7 Oct.) need rigorous dietary restrictions. You should avoid grilled dishes like BBQ, as well as foods with hot ingredients. Furthermore, while traveling or operating a car, you must constantly be aware and not be irresponsible, since you may sustain harm or bleed.

Chinese Astrology Horoscope for Each Month

Month 12 in the Rabbit Year (6 Jan 24 - 3 Feb 24) Your horoscope for people born in the Year of the Tiger has already begun to climb as we enter this month. However, the aftermath of issues and barriers persists. The main point is to keep your own system's working capital account under control. Furthermore, this month, avoid flaunting your face and attempt to lower your inflated ego. Increase your courtesy and humility. You should also assess your own work within the context of your own talents. This month is a financial outflow. There will be unanticipated costs, resulting in a shortage of money. Money from entertainment or some social gatherings, for example, will continue to flow out. As a result, if you have the ability to save, you should do so and eliminate needless costs. Keep a check on your finances and working capital to prevent going into the negative, and avoid being eager for high-risk investments because your expectations may not be satisfied. However, it resulted in property destruction and loss.

This month has been difficult in terms of work, especially business. You will be able to conquer it if you have the determination to endure and be patient. This year, though, you should follow the compromise concept. You should try to get help from both top and lower levels. In order to solve difficulties with collaboration and cooperation, because many heads are better than one.

Family horoscopes must be wary of those in their hometown who cause major squabbles. In terms of love, the relationship continues regularly, but with a happy side hidden.

In terms of health, there were no major illnesses or occurrences to be concerned about during this time period.

If you are trapped during this time, you will meet nice friends who will assist you.

Support Days: 3 Jan., 7 Jan., 11 Jan., 15 Jan., 19 Jan., 24 Jan., 27 Jan., 31 Jan.
Lucky Days: 12 Jan., 24 Jan.
Misfortune Days: 9 Jan., 21 Jan.
Bad Days: 6 Jan, 18 Jan. , 30 Jan

Month 1 in the Dragon Year (4 Feb 24 - 5 Mar 24)
Beginning this month, the path of your destiny became rocky and uneven. Thinking, reading, or any other activity should not be underestimated; one should not walk without caution.

There will be conflicts in the field of trade, and planning that still has loopholes will irritate you. As a result, increased scrutiny from all angles is required in various operations. Do not neglect those in command or ignore minor issues that arise. Large blunders can occur.

What you should do this month is concentrate on your work because the more you ignore it and dismiss it as unimportant, the longer you will leave it. There would be no easy way to unravel and end things.

This salary horoscope will have a property to lose. As a result, you should avoid betting on your luck. And if there is a criterion for investing in new things, caution should be increased.

There is no peace in the family because the members are suspicious of things they don't think they have until there are arguments and must be careful that the family will cause trouble.

In love, keep in mind that disagreements can lead to resentment, and avoid going to places of entertainment that can cause harm and trouble.

This month's health horoscope is for people suffering from liver disease, heart disease, or high blood pressure. Take special care of yourself and be wary of symptoms that will worsen. It's still not a good time to invest in new things.

Support Days: 4 Feb., 8 Feb., 12 Feb., 16 Feb., 20 Feb., 24 Feb., 28 Feb.
Lucky Days: 5 Feb., 17 Feb., 29 Feb
Misfortune Days: 2 Feb., 14 Feb. , 26 Feb
Bad Days: 11 Feb., 24 Feb.

Month 2 in the Dragon Year (6 Mar 24 - 5 Apr 24)
., 29 Feb.

Support Days: 3 Mar, 7 Mar., 44 Mar., 15 Mar., 19 Mar., 23 Mar., 27 Mar., 31 Mar.
Lucky Days: 12 Mar., 24 Mar.
Misfortune Days: 9 Mar., 21 Mar.
Bad Days: 6 Mar., 18 Mar., 30 Mar

Month 3 in the Dragon Year (6 Apr 24 - 5 May 24)
This month, your fortune is once again threatened by monsoon clouds. You should be wary of subordinates who cause problems and give you headaches. Furthermore, the destined one should be mindful of his own emotions, which frequently shift from good to evil, inflicting inadvertent harm to others. It will have an impact on work. As a result, you must be cautious with your own comments on this occasion. Do not brag, be confrontational, or spew vitriol at others, since this will put you in danger. All business activity must be conducted honestly. Don't cut corners or be greedy. It will cause more loss and harm than it will repair.

This month's financial situation is dire. It is sufficient to consider investing in gambling or speculating in numerous industries. However, once you have it, you must know when to quit and when enough is enough. Both should be more frugal with their expenditures. Always arrange your funds ahead of time. So that you do not end up being unable to reach your objective.

Be wary of subordinates or senior persons generating difficulty and maybe causing a huge number of money to be lost in families.

Many people will detest you if you adore them. Perhaps it's because you frequently appear dissatisfied and others avoid approaching you. If you go out and socialize late at night, you may get infectious illnesses as a result. This month, stay wary of accumulated stress that might lead to sleeplessness. You should also be cautious about the food you consume because it might cause injury and need the expenditure of funds for therapy.

Support Days: 4 Apr., 8 Apr., 12 Apr., 16 Apr., 20 Apr., 24 Apr., 28 Apr.
Lucky Days: 5 Apr., 17 Apr., 29 Apr
Misfortune Days: 2 Apr., 14 Apr., 26 Apr
Bad Days: 11 Apr., 23 Apr.

Month 4 in the Dragon Year (6 May 24 - 5 Jun 24)

When the Year of the Tiger begins this month, the destiny of the Year of the Tiger is on the rise. You have the potential to obtain fortune, popularity, and status, so you should organize your efforts for the entire year. But it will be a shame if there is a lack of preparation and means to pursue it. Furthermore, you should learn from the failures of the previous year and strive to grow.

This month involves cautious planning in terms of job and business. So you should be alert and calm. Every work activity that will be carried out should thoroughly consider the environmental factors before taking action. Because being reckless and hurried increases the likelihood of making a mistake and causing damage. In addition, an evil star will arise and center in your house of fate. As a result, anything you do must be transparent and in accordance with the country's laws.

The financial situation remains ordinary. Even if it's not great, it's not terrible. However, you must take the middle road of not being irresponsible by being thrifty and carefully budgeting your expenditures. Furthermore, if you want to gain money from gambling, you must be willing to assume a significant risk. Because fortune is a fickle thing. Be cautious; if you are overly greedy, you can become a victim of fraudsters.

There will be pandemonium inside the family during this time. Keep an eye out for burglars breaking into your home. Other security precautions should be taken. Additions and valuables should be stored safely.

The love horoscope is affected by winds and waves. There is always the possibility that someone you care about will alter their mind.

However, you have the option of changing your mind or continuing to love.

Health is in good shape. However, you must exercise caution because it might induce brain injuries and migraines.Frequent headaches can be caused by a lack of sleep or by being overly stressed. If you want to be healthy, you must take better care of yourself than you have in the past.

Support Days: 2 May, 6 May, 10 May, 14 May, 18 May, 22 May, 26 May, 30 May.
Lucky Days: 11 May., 23 May.
Misfortune Days: 8 May., 20 May.
Bad Days: 5 May., 17 May., 29 May.

Month 5 in the Dragon Year (6 Jun 24 - 6 Jul 24)
This month, the route of your life, born in the Year of the Tiger, goes to meet the shadows once more. Problems and impediments are met whether traveling forward or backward. Things that were once a problem resurface for you to repair with the same difficulties.

On this occasion, you should discuss and seek guidance from elders on a frequent basis. Don't isolate yourself and linger on your difficulties, which will lead to overthinking and distraction. Obstacles are things that force you to grow. Please don't be too concerned. However, you must identify and correct any defects in your work as soon as possible. Don't put it off any longer. During this time, you should do your utmost to carry out your responsibilities. If certain conditions exist, you must be patient and wait for time. You should be patient.

It's still not a good time to collaborate or invest at this point. If it is unavoidable, material should be thoroughly studied and screened.

This salary horoscope is in the middle. However, you should constantly preserve money in order to retain liquidity. Avoid lending money to others or signing guarantor agreements to assist anyone. You should also not bet, speculate, or do business that is likely to break local laws.

Fortunately, there is no mayhem to worry about on the family side. However, a married couple's lives is put to the test. For the destined who has yet to find their soul mate. May you control the world just by dedication and tenacity. However, you must maintain the beat and depart at the appropriate moment. Otherwise, you can consume water chestnuts. Please keep your heart hard and steady throughout this time if you already have a loved one. Do not give in to the power of incitement.

Support Days: 3 Jun., 7 Jun., 11 Jun., 15 Jun., 19 Jun., 23 Jun., 27 Jun.
Lucky Days: 4 Jun., 16 Jun., 28 Jun
Misfortune Days: 1 Jun., 13 Jun., 25 Jun
Bad Days: 10 Jun., 22 Jun.

Month 6 in the Dragon Year (7 Jul 24 - 7 Aug 24)
The horoscope of people born in the Year of the Tiger this month remains optimistic since they discovered the power of assistance to assist. On this occasion, you should plan and prepare for numerous aspects such as people, cash, plans, and work systems to be ready in order to

proceed to the scheduled destination. Starting a new career, buying stocks, and investing in other industries are all options. All have channels and excellent success rates. You should have solid human relations and create good relationships inside your team as well as with those with whom you must engage. Including business partners to build the route for a prosperous future.

You must have the confidence to grow or come out and invest during this moment of work, pushing forward and grasping prospects for a brighter future. Because this is a fantastic chance, you must be attentive and completely devoted. Whether you are expanding your business, branching out, developing a portfolio, or speeding your sales, you should act quickly and with the help of God.

This wage has vanished in terms of wealth. Please concentrate on earning a living while remaining honest with consumers and business partners. The lovely benefits will not vanish into thin air. You should not be irresponsible since investing too much can result in a shortage of liquidity in your operating capital. As a result, you should assess yourself based on your physical strength and financial means. The most essential thing this month is to not lend money or make assurances to anyone.

There is harmony in the household. On the surface, the love horoscope seems smooth. However, because there is still hidden secret power, you should act forcefully and be conscious of nurturing your heart correctly.

Good health If you become unwell, you will see a doctor who is knowledgeable in medicine and can assist you in recovering. This month's horoscope for family and friends is favorable. If you become trapped, you have a problem. You will make new acquaintances who will assist you in effectively resolving the situation.

Support Days: 1 Jul., 5 Jul., 9 Jul., 13 Jul., 17 Jul., 21 Jul., 25 Jul., 29 Jul.
Lucky Days: 10 Jul., 22 Jul.

Misfortune Days: 7 Jul., 19 Jul., 31 Jul.
Bad Days: 4 Jul., 16 Jul. , 28 Jul

Month 7 in the Dragon Year (8 Aug 24 - 7 Sep 24)

The fortunes of people born in the Year of the Tiger will improve this month. Because the path of life leads to the alliance line. An auspicious star was immediately observed circling and blazing brightly. Life is like to a fish seeking water. As a consequence, what you expect will have the desired conditions satisfied. Work will go well, and company will grow. What you should do on this occasion is take advantage of a fantastic chance that arises within this time period. You must act quickly and grasp it. Don't let it pass you by. Otherwise, others will come to help seize it instead, expediting the development of results, boosting sales, revenue, and new investments under favorable conditions, and compensating for the previous tough period.

Commerce and commercial wealth provide the way to success. As a result, I recommend that you start by cultivating love and harmony in your company. You will be able to work together to develop work and drive it toward the expected success goal. In addition, starting a new career, purchasing stocks, and making various investments. This time period has a positive view and outcome. You may choose your investment and enter at the right time for a big return.

In terms of fortune, this wage is abundant. There will be criteria for wage increases and promotions. Cash inflow comes in two forms: regular revenue and extra income from previously invested regions. Money from gambling and fortune all going through your hands to make you happy.

During this time, the family's horoscope finds serenity and no concerns. Love has a better outcome. It's an excellent moment to beg for love or make amends. Both have fortunate timing for a variety of auspicious occasions.

However, his health is deteriorating. You should limit your intake of fire element foods.

Be cautious of oral and gastrointestinal disorders, as well as toothaches, when grilling hot products or those with hot qualities.

Support Days: 2 Aug., 6 Aug., 10 Aug., 14 Aug., 18 Aug., 22 Aug., 26 Aug., 30 Aug
Lucky Days: 3 Aug., 15 Aug., 27 Aug
Misfortune Days: 12 Aug., 24 Aug.
Bad Days: 9 Aug., 21 Aug.

Month 8 in the Dragon Year (8 Sep 24 - 7 Oct 24)
This month, the path of your life has crossed a perilous chasm. Destiny's path is like being shook and rocked again, traveling in undulating lines. The destiny criterion change dramatically. As a result, on this occasion, you should: Be cautious and allow yourself to cool down first. Prepare your mind to face the inevitable issues. If you have been diligently preparing over the last month, This month will be lighter, but if you haven't prepared, you will face challenges throughout this month. Determine the root cause and put an end to it as soon as possible. Don't leave it hanging for

too long. Because it will spread much more widely.

This compensation is a squander of funds. As a result, you should not lend money to others or make financial assurances to assist others. Both outlaw gambling as well as gambling. When going out this month, be wary of pickpockets and misplaced belongings.

In terms of work and business, this is a time to be patient, calm, and in control of your emotions. Otherwise, numerous harmful effects will occur.

The family is concerned about having to spend money on medical expenditures for the elderly in the home.

This month, focus on your romantic side. You should use caution when speaking, as this might lead to misunderstandings or disputes.

During this time, health horoscopes frequently contain waist discomfort, back pain, and shoulder pain, and you must be wary of quiet ailments that may surface and request information. And this is again another month when travelers must prioritize safety above everything else.

This month, you should use caution while communicating with relatives and friends. since if you continue to talk without regard for the sentiments of the listener and are reluctant to disadvantage anybody in this manner, you will complicate your relationship since no one will give up on anyone else.
This month is not appropriate for starting a new career, investing in stocks, or making other types of investments.

Support Days: 3 Sep, 7 Sep., 11 Sep, 15 Sep, 19 Sep., 23 Sep., 27 Sep.
Lucky Days: 8 Sep, 20 Sep.
Misfortune Days: 5 Sep, 17 Sep. , 29 Sep
Bad Days: 2 Sep, 14 Sep. , 26 Sep

Month 9 in the Dragon Year (8 Oct 24 - 6 Nov 24)
This month's fortunes have not yet been spared the wrath of the rain. Personal issues are continuing causing continual upheaval. In such a case, you must have good control and know how to be cautious while staying alive. Do not interfere with other people's work or cause difficulties in order to increase pressure to yourself. There are certain things you should do this month, such as make time to exercise in order to enhance your immune system and overall health.

This month's direct income is satisfactory financially. However, you must still follow thrifty ideals. Some things can still be put off. Please be patient and do not rush to pay in order to avoid a lack of liquidity in the circulating system. Money from fortune is still fraught with danger. So don't hope in vain that you'll obtain it. Be wary of more significant issues than previously.

It is time to wait for the perfect timing and opportunity in terms of job and commerce. Be wary of interruptions to people in the organization or persons with whom you must interact. As a result, maintain and deepen relationships with those around you. It will assist you in overcoming this challenge.

Peace and good energies rule among the family. However, there are still misunderstandings in love, so avoid using emotion or being snarky. However, we must revise our understanding.

This is another month in which you must be cautious about being damaged by equipment and appliances. As a result, you should use caution.

Your relatives and friends appear to want to assist you, but they are unable to do so, therefore you must go on your own.

In terms of establishing a new career, joining stocks, and making other investments. This is not a good month. However, there are still certain channels in which you may invest and obtain rewards, more or less..

Support Days: 1 Oct., 5 Oct., 9 Oct., 13 Oct., 17 Oct., 21 Oct., 25 Oct., 29 Oct..
Lucky Days: 2 Oct., 14 Oct., 26 Oct
Misfortune Days: 11 Oct., 23 Oct.
Bad Days: 8 Oct., 20 Oct.

Month 10 in the Dragon Year (7 Nov 24 - 6 Dec 24)

The route of life for people born in the Year of the Tiger goes to meet the lucky star "Leng Tek" this month. The Dragon King's might aids in pushing forward and getting work back on track and running smoothly. Obstacles and issues from the previous month can be overcome. When other circumstances are quiet, you should do what you should do this month. You should review your previous blunders. Use prior experience and expertise to solve difficulties and resolve disagreements. Anything that has to be changed or relocated should be done as soon as possible. Always investigate and prepare yourself. In the event of unforeseen developments, you may need to prepare two or three backup plans. You will be able to adjust rapidly to the circumstance.

This month is going well in terms of work, especially commercial business. As a result, you should take advantage of this excellent chance to strengthen your dedication and endurance. Accelerate the implementation of outstanding initiatives, both in terms of outcomes and sales, so that actual results may be seen fast. Those around you will admire you for this. Commanders, in particular, will be able to see the intents. As a consequence, work will be able to go to the next level.

Even this month's financial situation will be mild. However, if you are really vigilant, your income will grow and vary proportionally, however you may not see the figures in this month's revenue account alone.

The family horoscope is serene. This month, you are likely to hear pleasant news or learn about the achievements of family members.

The haze has lifted on the love front. This month is a time for indulgent couples for singles. If you genuinely love each other and want to propose, go ahead and do it now because it is a favorable moment with a high likelihood of success.

Family and friends are helpful. Because, in addition to providing advise, he is also willing to assist you in resolving significant issues in your job.

This month is favorable for starting a new career or investing in stocks and other financial instruments. You can invest if you are willing to put up the first funds. It would be a pity to waste a good chance.

Support Days: 2 Nov., 6 Nov., 10 Nov., 14 Nov., 18 Nov., 22 Nov., 26 Nov ., 30 Nov
Lucky Days: 7 Nov., 19 Nov.
Misfortune Days: 4 Nov., 16 Nov., 28 Nov
Bad Days: 1 Nov., 13 Nov., 25 Nov

Month 11 in the Dragon Year (7 Dec 24 - 5 Jan 24)

Enter this month since the lucky stars are leaving. It has also moved through the channels of helpful partnerships. As a result, fortunes began to dwindle gradually. Problems and barriers that were evident from a distance began to arrive from all directions. They ran into unanticipated troubles at work and in their firm, which seemed to be going smoothly.

During this month, you should focus on difficulties that have already arisen. Arrange the priorities carefully, beginning with the most crucial issues and working your way down.

This month's work horoscope, particularly the commercial industry, is approaching a critical tipping point. You will also encounter people with evil motives who seek to intimidate and obstruct you, as well as readily having problems with your coworkers and supervisors. You should be wary of young people who cause disturbance and destruction, especially around this time of year. As a result, please be as careful as possible. Maintain job responsibilities while improving human relations abilities to cope with a variety of difficulties.

In terms of your fortune, your wage is still fluctuating. You must still be cautious of huge costs that may arise suddenly. You should budget your money in order to balance your income and spending. To avoid becoming immobilized and unable to proceed. Furthermore, do not gamble or sign any form of financial promise.

The family's circumstances are well at the moment. However, there are waves and disputes on the love front.

In terms of health, keep an eye out for bone discomfort, tendon pain, sleeplessness, and regular headaches caused by work stress. Please understand how to schedule adequate rest time.

Relatives and friends are not faring well. So let's focus on just three points. Unable to understand the heart of a friend who is actually tough to understand, be aware of certain friends who do not mean to be good and are considering betraying you.

Support Days: 4 Dec., 8 Dec., 12 Dec., 16 Dec., 20 Dec., 24 Dec., 28 Dec.
Lucky Days: 1 Dec., 13 Dec., 25 Dec.
Misfortune Days: 10 Dec., 22 Dec.
Bad Days: 7 Dec., 19 Dec., 31 Dec.

Amulet for The Year of the TIGER
"Three-Eyed God Ae Jiang removes danger"

This year, those born in the Year of the Tiger should create and revere spiritual artifacts. "Three-Eyed God Ia Jiang removes dangers" to improve your luck by setting it on your work or cash desk and asking for His grace to assist shield you from harm. Eliminate negative influences and threats to your destiny this year. You should seek his blessing to bring you money and abundance, as well as serenity and tranquillity in your future.

A chapter in the Department of Advanced Feng Shui discusses the gods who will come to reside in the mia keng (house of destiny) for the year. They are gods capable of bringing both good and terrible fortune to the god of fate in that year. When this is the case, worshiping to increase your luck with the gods who visit your birth year is said to be good and have the most influence on you. In order to rely on the gods' ability to defend you, There are calamities to relieve while your fortunes deteriorate.

At the same time, I'd want to pray for your blessing in order for my business to run well. Bring you and your family luck and success.

Yiang is the zodiac sign of those born in the Year of the Tiger or Mia Keng (destiny house). This year is expected to be quite fortunate for you. However, in order to work more than two jobs and avoid financial loss, you must be vigilant and work hard. You should avoid lending money to others or making promises to aid anyone, especially in July. In love, you will have to fight for her or fight for your guy with someone else. Common health issues this year include: headaches and sleeplessness, as well as taking precautions to avoid mishaps involving children in the home. If you intend to repair things, you should create a sacred object and wear an auspicious necklace in the shape of the "Three-Eyed God Ia Chiang, eliminating dangers" to petition Him for power and reputation. Promotes the intended person's job and business in order to provide success, progress, excellent health, and easy love. The family is content and contented.

"God Ae Jiang" or "God Yi Nueng Xing" was a brave and skilled celestial general. Capable of conquering adversaries in all three realms without fear. His distinguishing trait is the presence of a third eye on his forehead, which aids in the destruction of concealed adversaries and evil. He is also accompanied by the "Nine Tiang" (sky dog). As a result, the chosen individual and family members will be protected from threats such as numerous illnesses. Furthermore, if there is a problem with evil persons stealing property or money, and the establishment of religion. Having the "Three-Eyed God Ae Jiang Dispelling Disasters" in his possession will assist in dispelling all of these hazards.

Those born in the Year of the Tiger should also wear an auspicious jewelry. "Three-Eyed God Ae Jiang eliminates dangers." Wear it around your neck or keep it with you when you leave the house, both close and far. To complete your destiny with money and fortunate locations. Business and trade are flourishing and developing. The family is pleased all year, which leads to more efficiency and effectiveness, as well as speedier results than ever before.

Good Direction: Northeast, Northwest, and South
Bad Direction: North
Lucky Colors: Green, Blue, Gray, Black, and Blue.
Lucky Times: 11.00 – 11.59, 19.00 – 20.59, 21.00 – 22.59.
Bad Times: 09.00 – 10.59, 15.00 – 16.59, 23.00 – 00.59.

Good Luck For 2024

Printed in Great Britain
by Amazon